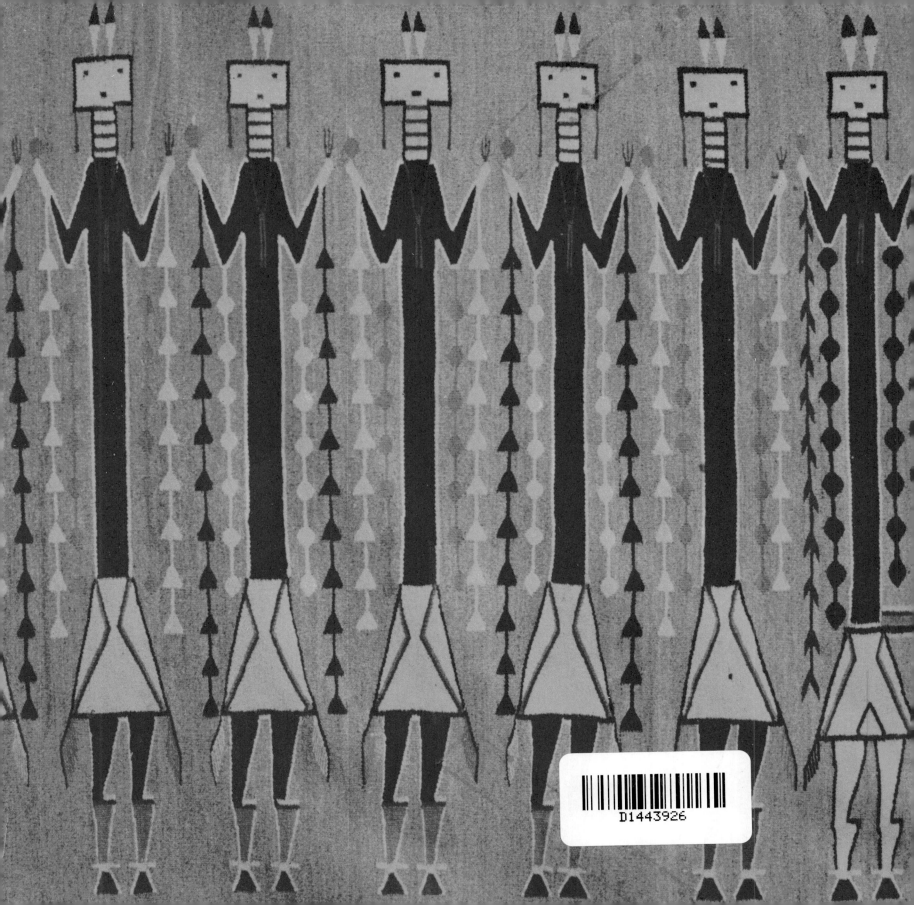

Front Cover:
Itapananánona kachina,
Zuñi, Brooklyn Museum

Endpapers:
Yei rug, Navajo, detail
Castle Hot Springs Collection

Back Cover:
Yei rug, Navajo,
Millicent A. Rogers Memorial Museum

Ramos polychrome pot,
Arizona State Museum,
University of Arizona

THE ART OF THE

SOUTHWEST INDIANS

Shirley Glubok

Photographs by Alfred Tamarin
Designed by Gerard Nook

The Macmillan Company, New York / Collier-Macmillan Limited, London

The author gratefully acknowledges the kind assistance of: *Robert G. Baker*, Chief Curator, Arizona State Museum, University of Arizona; *H. Thomas Cain*, Curator of Anthropology, The Heard Museum; *Allan Chapman*, Librarian, Museum of Primitive Art; *Richard Cònn*, Director, The Heard Museum; *Frederick J. Dockstader*, Director, Museum of the American Indian; *Nancy Fox*, Curator of Anthropology Collection, Museum of New Mexico; *Malcolm Hirsch*, Castle Hot Springs Hotel, Arizona; *Wilma Kaemlein*, Curator of Collections, Arizona State Museum, University of Arizona; *Richard W. Lang*, Curator, Museum of Navaho Ceremonial Art; *Ernest Leavitt*, Curator of Exhibits, Arizona State Museum, University of Arizona; *Toni S. Murphy*, Curator of Collections and Registrar, Maxwell Museum of Anthropology, University of New Mexico; *Carlos Nagel*, Director, Museum of New Mexico; *Bettina Smith*, Amerind Foundation; *Betty Toulouse*, Curator, Indian Arts Fund Collection, Museum of New Mexico; *Barton Wright*, Curator, Museum of Northern Arizona; *Dixie Yaple*, Director, and *John H. Yaple*, Curator, Millicent A. Rogers Memorial Museum; *Gail Heller;* and especially the helpful assistance of *George H. Ewing*, Associate Director, Museum of New Mexico

All photographs, with the exception of those on pages 4, 5, 7, 14, 17 and 46, left, are by Alfred Tamarin.

Other books by Shirley Glubok:

THE ART OF ANCIENT EGYPT
THE ART OF LANDS IN THE BIBLE
THE ART OF ANCIENT GREECE
THE ART OF THE NORTH AMERICAN INDIAN
THE ART OF THE ESKIMO
THE ART OF ANCIENT ROME
THE ART OF AFRICA
ART AND ARCHAEOLOGY
THE ART OF ANCIENT PERU
THE ART OF THE ETRUSCANS
THE ART OF ANCIENT MEXICO
KNIGHTS IN ARMOR
THE ART OF INDIA
THE ART OF JAPAN
THE ART OF COLONIAL AMERICA
THE FALL OF THE AZTECS
THE FALL OF THE INCAS
DISCOVERING TUT-ANKH-AMEN'S TOMB
DISCOVERING THE ROYAL TOMBS AT UR
DIGGING IN ASSYRIA
HOME AND CHILD LIFE IN COLONIAL DAYS

Dance wands, Hopi, wood,
Brooklyn Museum

Indian peoples have been living in the American Southwest for thousands of years. Long before the arrival of the first Europeans, they lived in what is now New Mexico and Arizona and in parts of present-day Colorado, Utah, California, Nevada and northern Mexico.

The Indian peoples of the Southwest belong to three main groups: the Pueblos, who have lived in villages for centuries; the Navajo and their close relatives the Apache; and the desert tribes, including the Pima, the Papago and the Mojave.

Today most of these Indians live on reservations, lands guaranteed to them by treaty with the United States government.

Rock pictures can be seen throughout the Southwest on the smooth surfaces of cliffs. Some are hundreds of years old. The meaning of these pictures is not fully understood, but it is thought that many had religious significance. Some rock pictures, called petroglyphs, are carved by cutting, scratching or chipping designs into the surface of the cliff. The ancient petroglyph above is on the reservation of the Zuñi, a Pueblo people, in New Mexico. It is filled with lively animal figures and geometric symbols.

Paintings on rock are called pictographs. They are usually found in caves and in shelters under overhanging rock shelves, where the paint was protected from rain and sun. The pictograph below, also on the Zuñi reservation, was painted in modern times. The paintings show masks used by the Zuñi in their ceremonies.

The sheer cliff walls of river valleys and canyons provided ancient Pueblo peoples with safe places in which to make their homes. One of these cliff dwellings, in Arizona, is called Montezuma's Castle. American settlers who mistakenly thought it had been built by the Aztec Indians from Mexico named it after the Aztec emperor, Montezuma.

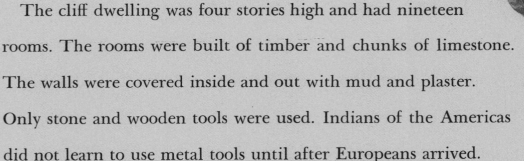

American Museum of Natural History

The cliff dwelling was four stories high and had nineteen rooms. The rooms were built of timber and chunks of limestone. The walls were covered inside and out with mud and plaster. Only stone and wooden tools were used. Indians of the Americas did not learn to use metal tools until after Europeans arrived.

The inhabitants of the cliff dwellings reached their homes by climbing ladders which could be pulled up in case of enemy attack. Montezuma's Castle had been abandoned long before the Spaniards arrived in the Southwest in 1540, searching for legendary cities of gold.

The Spanish conquerors found clusters of stone-and-mud houses, which they called *pueblos,* meaning "villages." Some were occupied; others were deserted. The largest, Pueblo Bonito in New Mexico, had about eight hundred rooms. The frog above, carved out of jet, comes from Pueblo Bonito.

Ancient people of southern Arizona carved the objects above. The birds, lizard and turtle are of shell, which was obtained through trade with Pacific Coast tribes.

Stone was used to make projectile points, the sharp, pointed tips of spears, darts and arrows. The arrowheads are made of jasper.

Small stone figurines of animals are used as fetishes, objects thought to have

supernatural powers that can protect their owners or bring them good luck.

The mountain sheep above is a prehistoric Zuñi fetish. The smooth planes in the

stone give the animal its form. The sheep's tail is coiled on its back.

The white onyx fetish below comes from a Pueblo community named Cochiti.

It has turquoise-stone eyes and strands of sinew wrapped around its body.

Objects such as arrowheads or feathers are often tied to the fetish to give it extra power.

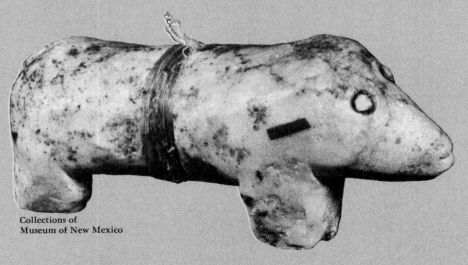

Basket-making is one of the oldest crafts in the Southwest. Bowls, jars and even water bottles and cooking vessels were woven by early basket-makers. A large variety of grasses, roots and stems, found everywhere, were used.

Museum of Northern Arizona

The Apache, who were nomads, favored baskets, because they are light, easily carried and do not break. The Apache storage basket at left is almost one hundred years old. It is decorated with figures of men and horses. Horses were unknown in America until the Spaniards brought them. The Apache became famous for their horsemanship. Today they raise horses and cattle.

Above, right, is an Apache basketwork bowl. The black designs were made from martynia, or devil's claw, a weed with unusually long spines.

The western Apache storage basket at right has the graceful shape and high shoulders of an olla, or water jar. It is very tightly woven and has an all-over net design with repeating human figures. The Apache were so well known for their baskets that one Apache tribe was named Jicarilla, which is Spanish for "little basket."

Arizona State Museum,
University of Arizona

11

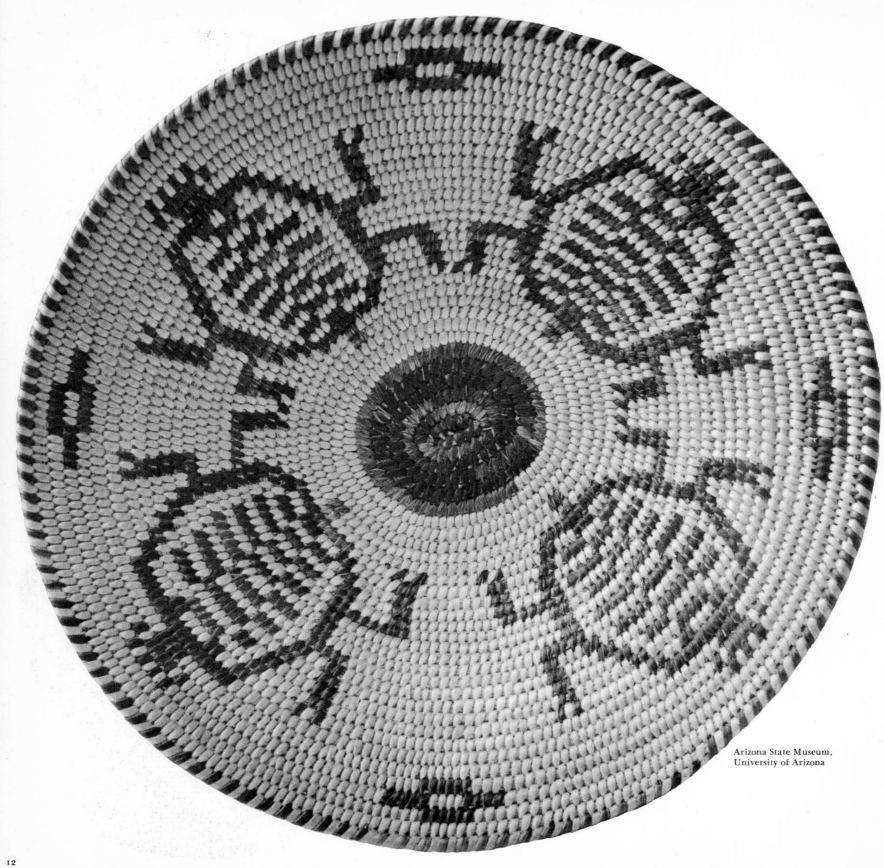

Arizona State Museum,
University of Arizona

One of the most popular methods of basket-making is coiling, a technique of building up a spiral of fiber to form the basket. Stiff reeds are used for the coils and more flexible grasses are used to sew the coils together.

Pima Indians favor willow twigs for their baskets, while the Papago use the yucca plant. A circular design of four turtles is woven into the flat Pima basket at left. The coils are smooth and even. They are sewn together with a slightly loose stitch.

A Papago basket-weaver made this doll-like figure which serves as a covered container. The arms, braids, eyes, mouth and nostrils have been sewn on. Papago craftsmen use the yucca in its natural green state, or bleach it white.

Arizona State Museum,
University of Arizona

*S*and paintings, believed to have magical healing powers, are made by the Navajo, the largest of all Indian nations. The sand painters are Navajo medicine men, also called singers. They chant ceremonial songs as they create traditional designs from memory. The paintings are made by carefully dropping dry pigments, powdered stone and charcoal on a bed of clean sand.

The ceremony takes place on the floor of a Navajo *hogan,* or house. The patient sits on the sand painting and is rubbed with the colored sands so that he will absorb the power of the Holy People in the painting.

According to Navajo legend, people came to this world (The Glittering World) from a dark world. The sand painting at left illustrates a Navajo concept of this world. The central figure, a symbol of moisture, is dressed in clouds and carries round baskets of earth from which plants sprout.

Close beside her are dontso bugs, guardian emblems. An otter and a beaver follow her footsteps. Over her head are dragonflies. Symbols of the ocean appear on either side. Above and below are frogs and turtles. The Navajo believe that as the singer chants his traditional song, the spirits who gave the painting and song to them come to see that the rites are being performed correctly. If they are, they will help the patient to become well again.

Emergence sand painting from the
Upward Reaching Ceremonial,
Collections of Museum of New Mexico

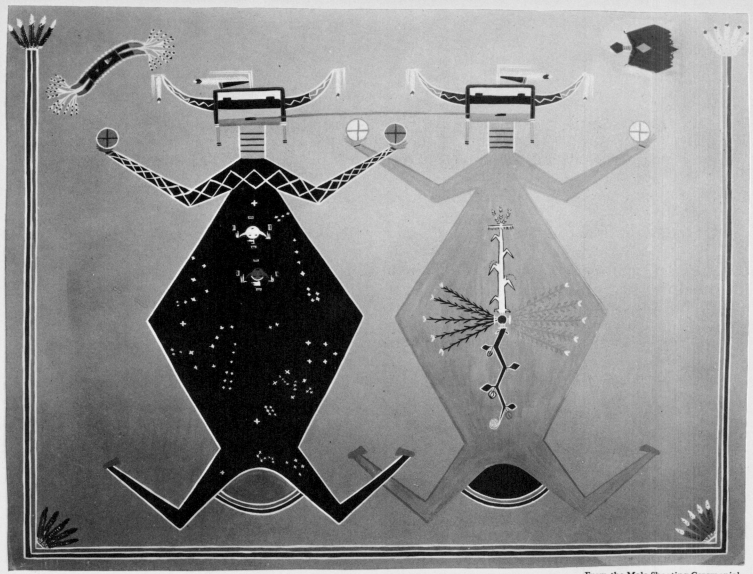

From the Male Shooting Ceremonial,
Museum of Navaho Ceremonial Art

The sand painting above shows the symbols of Father Sky and Mother Earth. Both

wear masks, as it is forbidden for anyone to see their faces. A line connects their

mouths, symbolizing affection between them.

The sun, moon and stars appear on the darker body of Father Sky. In the middle of Mother Earth's body is a circle representing a sacred lake with four holy plants emerging from it. A feathered rainbow guards three sides of the painting.

The painting at right, called *Bear Squatting Place,* is used to cure nervousness or fainting spells. The striped rainbow bars under the bears' feet show that the figures are moving. The rainbow bands coming out of their mouths represent their frightful roars and also form the trails along which bear tracks appear. The tracks above surround a black bears' den, crossed and encircled by rainbows.

Every sand painting is sacred and must be destroyed by sunset of the day it is begun. Any copy of a sand painting must be imperfect so that the Holy People will not be offended. There are more than four hundred traditional sand painting designs, each connected with a ceremony to cure illness or ward off danger.

From the Mountain Top Ceremonial, detail, Taylor Museum, Colorado Springs Fine Arts Center

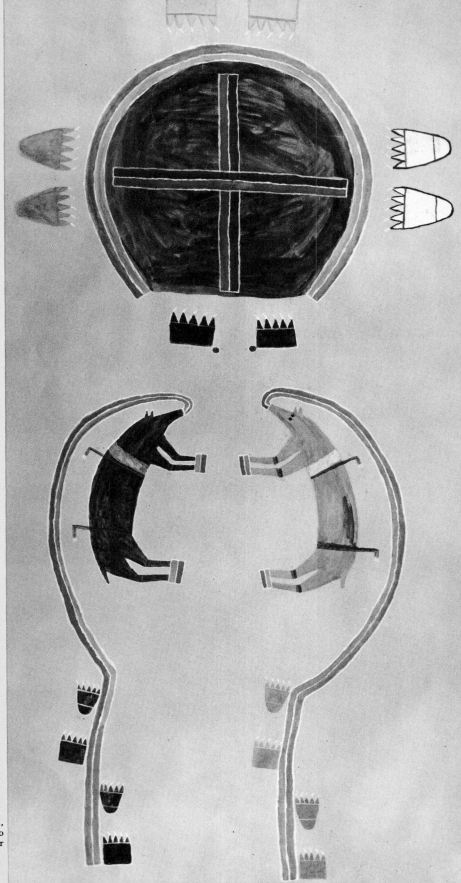

Kanachu kachina,
Brooklyn Museum

Pueblo people believe in spirit rainmakers, called *kachinas,* who live in mountains, clouds, springs and lakes. Long ago, according to legend, kachinas would come to the villages and dance for the people when they were lonesome or sad. The kachinas brought gifts and taught the people arts and crafts and how to hunt. They also danced in the fields to bring rain. One day a terrible fight broke out between the kachinas and the people, and the spirits refused to come back. However, they agreed to let the people wear ceremonial masks and costumes, paint their bodies and act as if they had become kachinas. There are many different kachinas, each identified by its mask. The masks are sacred.

These old masks came from the Zuñi pueblo. The one above is decorated with feathers and fur. The mask at right has a collar of spruce needles and a zigzag design which represents lightning.

Nahaliko (?) kachina,
Brooklyn Museum

Ohapa (?) kachina,
Brooklyn Museum

Saiyatasha kachina,
Millicent A. Rogers
Memorial Museum

Kachina masks are made of deer or buffalo hide. The Zuñi mask at left has a big beak and diamond-shaped eyes. The leather strings hold it in place. The mask above is called Long Horn, because of its single blue horn. One of its eyes is bigger than the other. Long Horn is especially loved by the Zuñi. The mask's long horn and long eye bring long life to all of its people. The hair is bear fur, topped with feathers.

Kachina masked dances are still performed in the pueblos during the first six months of every year. An important part of the dancing ceremonies is the presentation of gifts to the children.

Supai kachina, Heard Museum,
courtesy Fred Harvey Foundation

Shalako Maiden kachina,
Heard Museum, courtesy
Fred Harvey Foundation

Fathers and uncles of the little Pueblo children carve kachina dolls which are distributed as gifts during the dances. The children take the dolls home to remind them about the many different kachina spirits. The dolls are not toys, yet the children are permitted to play with them.

Kachina dolls of the Hopi Indians of Arizona are carved out of wood from the roots of dead cottonwood trees. The body is made from one solid block. Horns, headdresses, noses and ears are attached separately. The costumes of the Hopi kachinas are painted on in fine detail. These old kachina dolls are stiff and simply carved, with mere stumps for legs. The one above wears a mask with a huge headdress. The mask on the kachina at left has horns on the sides of its head.

Today the Hopi make kachinas showing the dancers in action. The arms and legs stand out from the body, and the knees are bent.

Not all of the kachinas are friendly. The Black Ogre punishes those who break the ceremonial or social law. At left is a Black Ogre kachina doll holding a knife and a stick which make him more frightening. His kilt, or skirt, is painted on, but the animal skin across his shoulder and the fringe on his legs are of real leather.

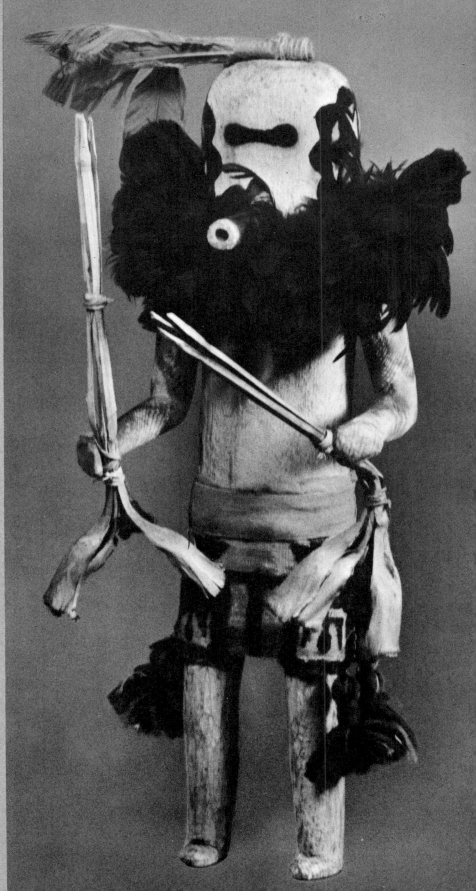

Zuñi kachinas are usually taller and thinner than Hopi ones. The arms are carved separately and attached so that they are articulated, or movable.

The Zuñi kachinas are dressed in costumes of painted cloth, fur, feathers, lamb's wool and buckskin. Old Zuñi kachinas are of pine. The one at right wears a cloth kilt and a collar of black feathers. He holds sticks of vegetable fibers to show that he is a seed gatherer.

Kohánona kachina, Brooklyn Museum

Overleaf, left to right: Red Fox kachina and Marau kachina, Hopi, Heard Museum, courtesy Fred Harvey Foundation; Zuñi kachina, Brooklyn Museum; Honani (badger) kachina, Hopi, Heard Museum, courtesy Fred Harvey Foundation

ndians in the Southwest made ceremonial robes of whole animal skins. These buckskin or deer hides were decorated with painted figures. The hides were prepared by putting them in damp sand or soaking them in water until the hair was loosened. Then the skins were scraped, stretched and rubbed smooth. The Zuñi robe at left is painted with a representation of a hunt. The lines reaching from the mouths of the animals to their interiors and ending in an arrow point are called heart lines, a typical feature of Zuñi painting. Black paint was obtained by boiling the sumac plant.

Millicent A. Rogers Memorial Museum

The Knife-Winged Monster, a mythical figure with a man's body and bird's wings, who captures women and carries them into the sky, is painted on the Zuñi robe at right. Arched over his head is his bow, the rainbow.

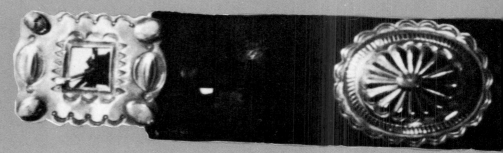

For the past hundred years the Navajo have been master silversmiths. They learned the art of working silver from Mexicans living nearby. Among the earliest silver ornaments were bells hammered out of twenty-five cent pieces. Navajo men wore the bells tied to their garters when they danced. Silver dimes, quarters and half dollars were used to make buttons and were also melted down for jewelry, until the defacing of coins was prohibited by the United States Government.

At left is a Navajo "squash blossom" necklace. The crescent in the center, called a *nahja,* was a magic amulet to ward off the Evil Eye. The nahja

was often used as the centerpiece of a horse's bridle.

Early Navajo silversmiths made tobacco canteens for United States soldiers stationed in army posts in the Southwest. To make the canteens the silversmiths hammered out two round sheets of silver and soldered, or joined them together with melted metal. The designs were stamped on.

Navajo men wore leather straps on their wrists to protect them from the snap of the bowstring when they shot an arrow. Today these bow-guards, or *ketohs,* are worn only for dress occasions.

The old Navajo belt above has scalloped conchas alternating with silver butterfly shapes.

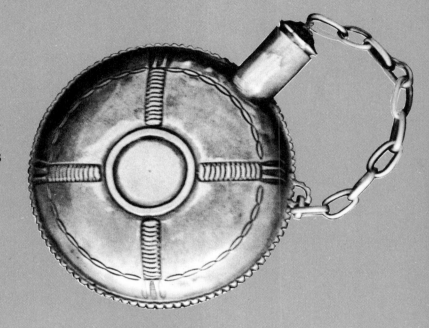

Maxwell Museum of Anthropology,
University of New Mexico

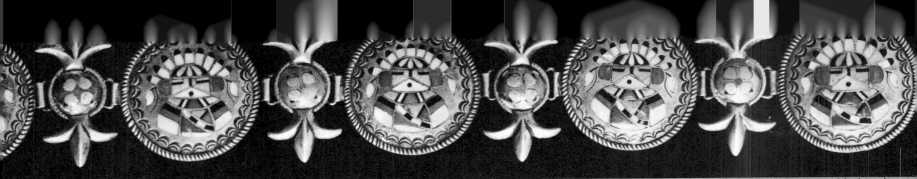

Concha comes from the Spanish word meaning "shell." The Navajo began to make concha belts after seeing the silver ornaments worn by enemy tribesmen of the Great Plains.

The modern concha belt above is a link-type; the round silver conchas and alternating butterflies are attached directly to each other. The raised designs on the conchas are made by hammering the silver on the reverse side. This method of metalwork is called repoussé. The butterflies are formed by sand-casting, a method of making jewelry by carving the shape in a block of sandstone to create a mold.

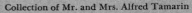

Molten silver is then poured into the hollow area.

The belt was made by a Zuñi silversmith. The Zuñi learned silversmithing from the Navajo. Zuñi craftsmen use large quantities of semiprecious stones, especially turquoise, carefully cutting the stones and setting them into the silver. Each of the conchas in this belt is inlaid with a design of turquoise, jet, shell and coral.

The Knife Wing pendant at left, below, is also inlaid with turquoise, jet, shell and coral. Droplets of silver form the wing and tail feathers. Curls of silver wire are laid over the ears.

Indian men and women in the Southwest wear all the bracelets they own at one time, along with all the other jewelry they possess. The Zuñi bracelet, above right, is set with beautifully cut turquoise stones in a sunburst pattern, bordered by slender twists of silver. Drops of silver are embedded between the stones.

The circular pin at center right is also in a sunburst design. Thin rows of twisted wire with crescent shapes and stars are soldered on the bracelet shown at bottom right. Each of the hundred stones is set separately, in bezels, the little prongs of silver which hold them in place.

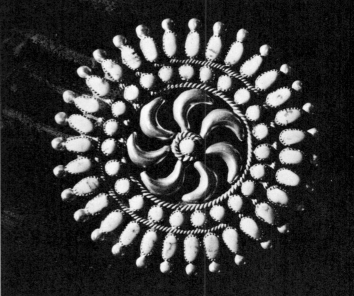

Collection of Mr. and Mrs. Alfred Tamarin

Navajo rugs have become famous as symbols of the Southwest. At first the Navajo wove blankets for clothing. Now they weave colorful wall hangings and floor coverings as well. Navajo weavers are women.

Among the Pueblos the men do the weaving. The Pueblos wove cotton long before the Spanish arrived. The Spaniards brought with them five thousand sheep which had long, straight wool. Then weaving with wool became widespread.

The Navajo learned weaving from the Pueblos in the early nineteenth century. All the work on Navajo rugs from the carding, or combing, of the wool, spinning of the thread and preparation of the dyes to the weaving itself is done by hand. The Navajo weave on upright looms. The warp, or foundation threads, are strung up and down. The weft, or horizontal threads, are woven through the warp threads to create the designs.

Early Navajo weavers made use of natural wool colors: brown, black, gray and white. They also made colors from vegetable dyes. Later weavers favored factory-made aniline dyes, and traders introduced commercial yarns which proved popular. The Navajo also used machine-woven cloth which they unraveled and respun. A favorite was bayeta, a wool cloth known for its vivid red dye made from the cochineal bug. The rug at right and the saddle blanket at left are woven with geometric patterns.

Castle Hot Springs Collection

Designs in Navajo weaving are memorized and passed on from mother to daughter. The earliest designs were simple stripes. Then a zigzag pattern was developed and diamond shapes also became popular. As time went on, rugs were

Castle Hot Springs Collection

woven with pictorial figures. Sometimes designs were taken from sand paintings.

Slender figures of supernatural beings called Yeis are woven into the rug at left. Curving around the four Yei figures is the Rainbow Goddess. The pictorial rug at right represents the Navajo spirit figure Big Fly.

The Navajo continue to weave rugs today, even though the practice of weaving by hand is slow and difficult. Modern weavers are even returning to natural vegetable dyes, instead of using factory-made products.

Castle Hot Springs Collection

The Mescalero Apache of Arizona hold tribal ceremonies each July for the young girls of the tribe who have reached womanhood. The ceremonies continue for four days and four nights. Every night men impersonate Mountain Spirits, who live in caves beneath the horizon to the north, east, south and west. They dance around a roaring bonfire.

The dancers paint their bodies. They wear black cloth masks and elaborate crowns of painted cottonwood sticks decorated with feathers.

The dances are part of a ritual to ward off evil. The vigorous gestures of the dancers make this spectacle one of the most exciting of all Indian ceremonies. These doll figures of the dancers are made for trade. They have no ceremonial purpose.

Pottery-making has been practiced by Indian women in the Southwest for hundreds of years. The Hohokam, ancestors of some of the modern desert tribes, created this pottery figure in the shape of a big-horned mountain sheep. The clay, a natural buff color, was decorated with red mineral paint, made from iron oxide.

The black-on-white vessel in the shape of a macaw is a canteen, with a small opening in the head for drinking. The macaw, a species of parrot, is not native to the Southwest. The birds were obtained by trade with Indians of Central America.

The black-on-white bowl, at right, with an antelope decoration was made by people in the Mimbres River Valley. Mimbres bowls are found in graves, placed

Arizona State Museum, University of Arizona

over the heads of people who had made and used them. It was believed that a vessel contained the spirit of its maker, so at the time of his burial a hole was punched into it to release the spirit.

These pots come from ancient sites in Arizona, and are at least 750 years old.

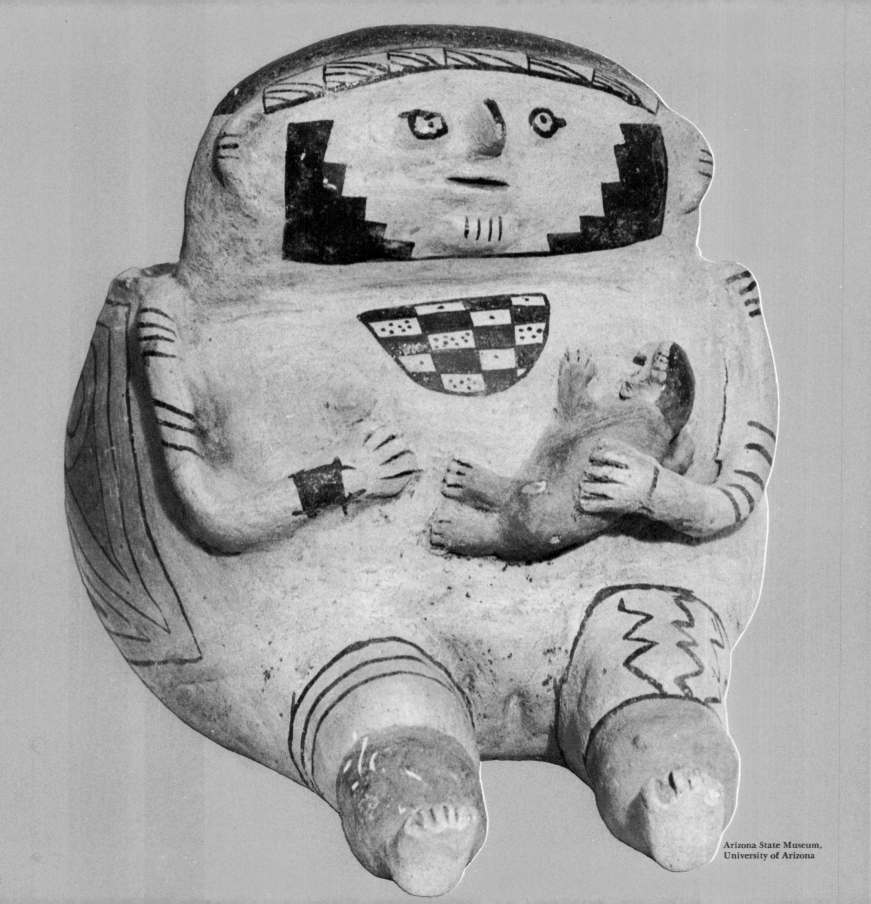

42

Amerind Foundation

Pottery painted with more than two colors is called polychrome. This polychrome jar in the form of a mother nursing a baby comes from the area of northern Mexico that is now the state of Chihuahua. The jar is more than five hundred years old. A high-quality clay which can be delicately modeled is found in the area. The head of the figure extends above the opening of the jar.

The mug above looks modern in form but is actually about seven hundred years old. The ancestors of modern Pueblos probably made it for drinking and it may also have served as a dipper.

Pueblos living in the last century modeled this odd polychrome pot, with its painted face. We do not know what it was used for. It may have been made just for fun.

Museum of Northern Arizona

Maxwell Museum of Anthropology,
University of New Mexico

44

Today, the thinnest-walled pottery in the Southwest is made in the pueblo of Acoma in New Mexico. The Acoma pot at left is a water jar. Acoma potters paint their vessels with all-over patterns of sweeping curves and sharp angles. Birds with spread tail feathers are a typical motif.

Ancient polychrome designs were used to decorate the modern pot above, right. The vessel was made and signed by Fannie Nampeyo, a descendant of Nampeyo, a famous Hopi potter.

The graceful pottery jar, below right, was produced in the Cochiti pueblo. Curved lizard forms were modeled separately and applied to the jar.

Maxwell Museum of Anthropology, University of New Mexico

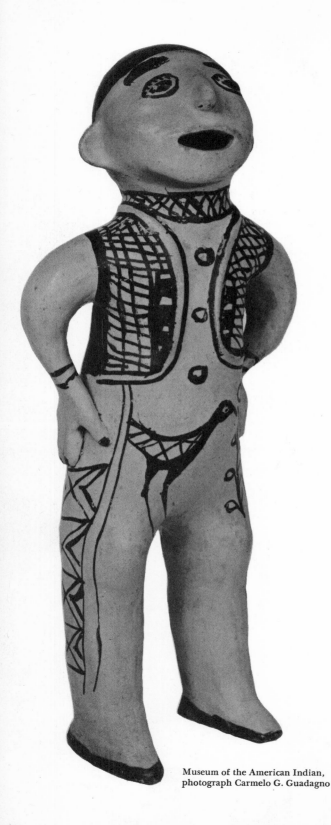

ochiti potters model clay figurines of fish, animals and people. This male figure is simply formed. His features and clothes are painted on.

The pottery jar below, decorated with flying birds, was made in a New Mexican pueblo, Zia. The owl at right, below, holding two fledglings is a Zuñi pot.

The Mojave Indians, who live in Arizona and southern California, made the vessel at right, above, with four spouts and a human head. It is decorated with real earrings and a bead necklace.

Museum of the American Indian,
photograph Carmelo G. Guadagno

Maxwell Museum of Anthropology,
University of New Mexico

46

Modern Indian pottery-making in the Southwest continues ancient traditions. Pottery is still shaped without using the potter's wheel. The method most often practiced is coiling. Lumps of clay are rolled into ropes which are placed one on another to form the walls of the vessel. The pot is usually scraped smooth with a piece of dried gourd, and polished with a stone. The vessel is then fired or baked.

Slip, or liquid clay, is usually applied to the pot to smooth the surface, and paint is added before firing.

Most of the paints are made from finely ground minerals mixed with water. The color black can be produced by boiling bee weed, a plant which grows high in the mountains, until it becomes a thick paste.

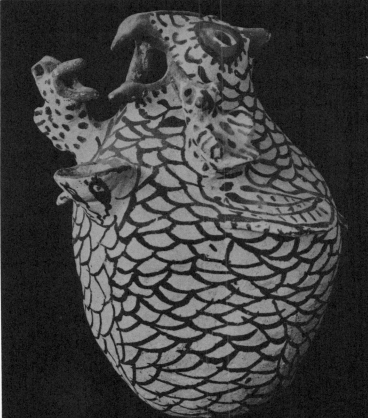

Pottery with geometric designs is still being made by the Maricopa Indians of Arizona. One of the leading Maricopa potters, Ida Redbird, made and signed this bowl. She uses the methods she learned from her ancestors and is teaching them to her grandchildren and great-grandchildren.

Today, art still flourishes among the Indians of the Southwest. The different Indian peoples in the region follow many of the traditions of their ancestors. They have also adopted arts and crafts practiced by other Indian groups and by the Spaniards, Mexicans and Americans. The Southwest Indians are proud of their art. The Navajo, the Apache; the Hopi, the Zuñi and the other Pueblos; the Pima, Papago, Mojave and other desert tribes: all are teaching their children to carry on this heritage.

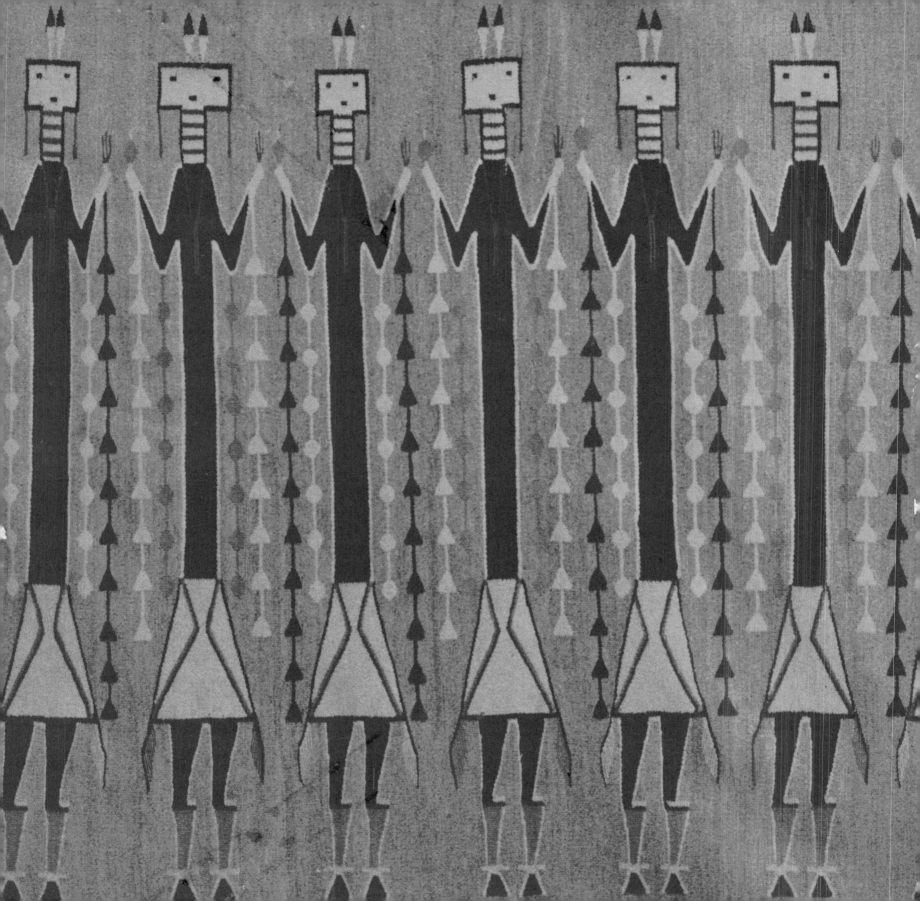